The Nature Kid's Guide to
MUSKRATS

DAVID ANDERSON

LP Media Inc. Publishing
Text copyright © 2026 by LP Media Inc.
All rights reserved.

For information address LP Media Inc. Publishing,
30012 Variolite St NW, Princeton MN 55371
www.lpmedia.org

Publication Data

Muskrats
The Nature Kid's Guide to Muskrats — First edition.

Summary: "Learn all about Muskrats, the Nature Kid Way"
— Provided by publisher.

ISBN: 979-8-89818-246-5

[1. Muskrats – Non-Fiction] I. Title.

Title: The Nature Kid's Guide to Muskrats

CONTENTS

MUDDY MARSHES

4

Splash! A furry muskrat slips off the bank into a marsh.

Somewhere in a quiet **marsh**, a pair of eyes breaks the surface of the water. A sleek brown shape glides forward without a sound. Meet the muskrat, one of North America's most capable and overlooked wild animals.

Muskrats are built for wetland life. Marshes, ponds, and slow-moving streams are their territory. Cattails sway overhead, soft mud lines the bottom, and the water itself keeps them cool and safe from danger.

For a muskrat, a healthy marsh is not just a nice place to live. It has everything it needs to survive.

MAP MAKERS

After escaping into the wild in Europe in the early 1900s, muskrats spread across the entire continent in less than 50 years!

Whoosh! A muskrat paddles down a cold northern stream.

Muskrats live all across North America. You can find them from cold Canada down to warm Mexico. They are one of the most common wetland animals in the United States.

Long ago, people brought muskrats to Europe for their fur. The muskrats escaped and spread fast. Now they live wild in Europe and parts of Asia too.

Muskrats are remarkably adaptable. Slow rivers, mountain lakes, roadside ditches, and city ponds have all become home to muskrats willing to make the best of whatever water they can find.

SMALL STUFF
FUN FACT!
A muskrat can squeeze through any hole as wide as its own head!

Squish! A muskrat squeezes through a narrow gap in the reeds.

A muskrat is about the size of a big guinea pig. It weighs two to four pounds—about as heavy as a small bag of sugar.

From nose to tail, a muskrat measures close to two feet long. Half of that length is its thin, scaly tail! The body itself is round and plump.

A muskrat looks a bit like a tiny beaver. But beavers are much, much bigger. One adult beaver can weigh ten times as much as a muskrat!

TERRIFIC TAILS

10

Swish! A muskrat swings its long, scaly tail through the water.

A muskrat's tail is not like other rodent tails. It is flat on the sides and covered in tiny scales. Very little fur grows on it.

The tail works like a **rudder** on a boat. It helps the muskrat steer when it swims. A push left or right changes its path through the water instantly.

On land, the tail drags behind on the ground. It leaves a wavy line in soft mud between two tiny paw prints. Look for this mark near the water's edge!

WHISKER
WONDERS

FUN
FACT!

A muskrat's nose snaps
shut like a tiny door when it
dives underwater!

12

Flick! A muskrat's whiskers twitch at a tiny ripple in the water.

Muskrats have long whiskers on their snout. These stiff hairs help them feel things in the dark. Even in murky water, they know exactly what is near.

Under the surface, it is hard to see. Whiskers pick up small waves and movements, helping muskrats find food and avoid danger. Each whisker sends signals straight to the brain.

Muskrats have small ears that close tight when they dive. Their sense of smell is very strong too. All these senses work together to keep them safe.

HIDE WELL

DID YOU KNOW?
Some muskrat tunnels have a hidden back exit just for emergency escapes!
14

Shhhh! A muskrat holds perfectly still in the thick brown reeds.

Brown fur helps muskrats blend in with the world around them. Their coat looks just like mud and dead plants. Spotting them from far away is very hard.

When danger is close, muskrats stay perfectly still. They crouch low in the reeds and freeze. A hawk might fly right over and never see them hiding below.

Some muskrats dig tunnels in riverbanks instead of building lodges. The opening is always hidden under the water. This secret entrance keeps them safe from animals on land.

MUNCHY MUSKRATS
DID YOU KNOW?
A hungry muskrat can eat one third of its body weight every single day!

Crunch! A muskrat bites into a thick, juicy cattail stem.

Muskrats eat lots of plants. Cattails are a top favorite. They also munch on water lilies, rushes, and pond weeds.

To eat, a muskrat sits on a log or mat of floating plants. It holds food in its small front paws and nibbles away. One muskrat can munch for hours at a time.

Sometimes muskrats eat small animals too. Clams, snails, and tiny fish make tasty treats. But plants make up about ninety percent of what they eat each day.

SQUEAKY SOUNDS
FUN FACT!
Muskrats can squeak to each other even while swimming underwater!
18

Squeak! A muskrat calls out from just outside its dark tunnel.

Muskrats make soft squeaks and chirps to talk to each other. A mother may squeak to call her babies close. Loud squeals can warn that danger is near.

Muskrats also use smell to share news. They make a musky oil near their tails and rub it on rocks and logs. This scent marks their territory.

The musky smell warns other muskrats to stay away. It marks the edges of a family's home area. That strong, oily scent is how muskrats got their name!

DANGER
ZONE

DID YOU KNOW?
A great horned owl can snatch a muskrat in total darkness using only its hearing!

Screech! A hawk swoops down. The muskrat runs to dive back into the pond.

Many animals hunt muskrats. Hawks, owls, and eagles swoop down from above. Foxes and coyotes chase them on land.

Mink are one of the biggest dangers. A mink is small and slim enough to follow a muskrat right into its tunnel.

Snapping turtles hunt them from below the water.

In winter, there are fewer plants to hide behind. Muskrats must watch out at all times. Life in the wild can be tough for these small swimmers.

DIVE DEEP

FUN
FACT!

A diving muskrat can slow its
heartbeat to save oxygen while
hiding underwater!

Plop! A muskrat drops under the surface and disappears fast.

When danger comes, muskrats dive fast. They can vanish below the surface in less than one second. The dark water hides them right away.

Muskrats hold their breath for a very long time. They can stay under for up to fifteen minutes! This gives them plenty of time to swim far from any danger.

Sometimes a muskrat pops up on the other side of the pond. It surfaces far from where it went under. The confused hunter never knows where it went.

SWIM STRONG

Muskrats swim under frozen ice all winter, navigating dark freezing water to reach their food!

Swoosh! A muskrat zooms through the water like a tiny speedboat.

Muskrats are powerful swimmers. Their back feet are partly **webbed** like duck feet. This helps them push through water with surprising speed.

Stiff hairs grow along the edges of their toes. These hairs act like tiny paddles, and each kick sends the muskrat shooting forward.

Muskrats can swim both forward and backward. They can also float on top without moving a muscle. Thick fur traps air bubbles and keeps them bobbing like corks.

BUSY BODIES

A muskrat may spend up to six hours each day just searching for food!

Scratch! A muskrat grooms its thick, wet fur on the muddy bank.

Muskrats are busiest at dawn and dusk. They rest during the hottest part of the day. When the sun sinks low, they come out to eat and explore.

Grooming takes up a lot of time. Muskrats use their sharp claws to comb through their fur carefully. Clean fur stays waterproof and keeps them warm in cold water.

Muskrats also spend hours gathering plants. They carry bundles of reeds back to their home. There is always something to do in the busy marsh.

LODGE LIFE

FUN FACT!
Some muskrat lodges stand three feet tall and are used by families for many years!

Thump! A muskrat packs more mud onto the top of its lodge.

Muskrats build **lodges** out of plants and mud. A lodge is a big, round pile that sits in the water. Inside there is a dry room above the water line where the family sleeps.

A muskrat family shares one lodge together. Mom, dad, and their young all live inside. In cold weather, they huddle close to stay warm.

Some lodges have more than one room inside. Tunnels lead in and out from under the water. The family keeps adding to their lodge all year long, making it bigger and stronger.

SPRING SWEETIES

Some muskrat pairs can have up to five litters of babies in just one year!

Chirp! A male muskrat calls out to a female across the pond.

Spring is mating time for muskrats. The days grow longer and warmer. Males start looking for a mate.

A male swims from pond to pond searching for a female. He may travel far from his home territory. Males sometimes fight each other, biting and wrestling over a female.

Once a pair meets, they stay close together. They swim side by side and touch noses gently. Soon the female will be ready to have her babies.

TINY KITS

DID YOU KNOW?
A newborn muskrat kit weighs less than one ounce—lighter than a slice of bread!

Peep! A tiny, pink muskrat kit wiggles next to its brothers and sisters.

Baby muskrats are called **kits**. They are born tiny, with no fur and with their eyes shut tight. Each kit is only about the size of a grape.

A litter can have four to eight kits at a time. They are born inside the lodge where it is safe and warm. The kits snuggle close to their mother.

In just two weeks, the kits open their eyes. Soft brown fur starts to grow in. They gain weight fast and are soon ready to explore the world outside.

MOM MATTERS

DID YOU KNOW?
A mother muskrat carries her babies gently in her mouth to move them to safety!

Sniff! A muskrat mother licks her young kit all over.

Mother muskrats take great care of their kits. They nurse them with rich milk many times a day. This helps the babies grow big and strong quickly.

Mom also keeps the lodge tidy and clean. She brings in fresh plants for soft bedding. Warm, dry bedding helps her little kits stay healthy.

After about four weeks, mom takes the kits to the water for the first time. She shows them how to swim and find food. By six weeks old, the young muskrats can care for themselves.

SUPER SURVIVORS

36

Crack! A muskrat wades through an icy stream in winter.

Muskrats are tough survivors. They live through hot summers and freezing winters. They do not hibernate or move away when it gets cold.

In winter, food is hard to find, but muskrats know exactly where to look. They dig through frozen mud for roots and stems buried at the bottom of the pond. Air pockets trapped under the ice help them breathe between dives.

Muskrats also help the places they live in. When they eat old plants, new ones can grow. Healthy marshes are good for fish, birds, and many other animals too.

SPOT THEM

Look for chewed cattail stems floating near the shore—that means muskrats are close by!

Rustle! A muskrat glides across the quiet pond near the reeds.

Want to spot a muskrat in the wild? Head to a pond or marsh with cattails. Find a good spot to sit and watch quietly. Stay low and keep your eyes on the water.

Look for a V-shaped wave on the surface. A swimming muskrat makes this shape as it moves. You might also spot one sitting on a rock or bank, munching on plants.

Stay very quiet and hold perfectly still. Muskrats will swim away if they hear you coming. Be patient, and you may spot one up close!

GLOSSARY

marsh

A low, wet area where many plants grow

lodge

A muskrat's home made of mud and plants

kit

A baby muskrat

webbed

Having thin skin between the toes for swimming

rudder

A flat part that steers something through water